Afraid

A Cherrytree Book

Designed and produced by
A S Publishing

First published 1990
by Cherrytree Press Ltd
Windsor Bridge Road
Bath, Avon BA2 3AX

British Library Cataloguing in Publication Data
Amos, Janine
  Afraid.
  I. Title II. Green, Gwen III. Series
  823.914 (J)

ISBN 0-7451-5097-7

Printed and bound in Italy by New Interlitho, Milan

Afraid

By Janine Amos
Illustrated by Gwen Green

CHERRYTREE BOOKS

Tony's story

One night Tony couldn't get to sleep. His head was full of ideas. Mostly he was thinking about a ghost he'd seen in one of his comics. The more he thought about the picture, the harder it was to get to sleep.

Tony tossed and turned. He opened his eyes and looked around the dark room. What was that shape in the corner? Tony started to feel afraid.

It seemed to Tony that something else was in the bedroom too, but it was too dark to see. Could he hear it breathing?

Tony slid right down under the covers.

"Mum! I don't feel well," he shouted.

Tony's mum switched on the bedroom light. Tony saw his own, safe bedroom all around him and he felt much better.

"What's the matter, Tony?" asked his mum. But Tony didn't want to tell her.

"Well, I expect you were dreaming," she said as she went through the door. "Go back to sleep now."

"Don't shut the door!" called Tony. "Leave it open a bit, please - just in case I feel ill again." Tony could see the light outside his door and he wasn't afraid.

Why didn't Tony tell his mum how he was feeling?
How do you think his mum felt at this moment?

The next day Tony had a great time. He played football with his friends. But when his bedtime came, Tony said that he didn't feel tired.

"Go upstairs with a book, then," said his mum. "You'll soon fall asleep."

"Let me just watch this programme on TV," said Tony.

Then Tony wanted a drink. Then he wanted to clean his football boots.

"Enough!" said his mum. "Go to bed. Now!"

Tony trailed upstairs. When he got into bed he left the door open, with the light on outside. It was late. Soon his mum went to bed too, and she put off all the lights.

Tony lay in the dark. Things seemed to be moving in the room. Was it the ghost? Tony couldn't keep still. He jumped out of bed and put on the light.

If you were Tony, what would you do now?

Tony looked round his room. All his things were just as he'd left them. There was nothing unusual or bad about the room. He went back to bed. After a while, he fell asleep with the light on.

When Tony woke in the morning, his brother Pete was sitting on the bed. He gave Tony a glass of orange.

"You left your light on all night," said Pete. "Was there a reason?" Tony went red.

"I must have forgotten," he lied.

"Listen, Tony," said Pete. "It doesn't matter. Lots of people get scared of the dark sometimes. I was for a while."

"Were you?" asked Tony. "I know it's silly, but I really did think there was something in my room. I'm afraid of the dark." Tony started to cry.

"You won't be afraid tonight, I promise," said Pete. "We can do something about it, now that I know."

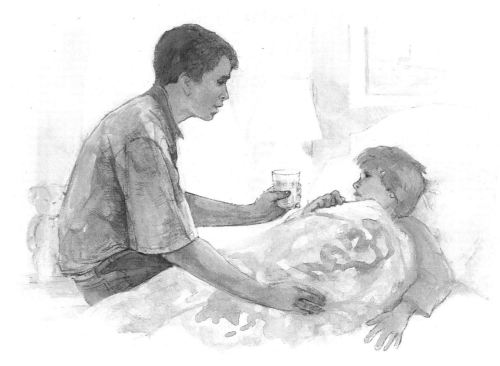

That night when Tony went to bed, Pete went with him.

"Tell me about the thing in your room," said Pete. "Was it green and hairy?"

"No," said Tony. "It's grey." He showed Pete the comic.

"Oh, him!" said Pete. "I saw him just now in the bathroom. He was cleaning his teeth ready for bed."

Tony grinned. His brother always made him laugh. But it made him feel better. He climbed into bed giggling.

"I'll leave your door open," said Pete, "and the hall light on - so the ghost can see its way!" Tony giggled, and soon fell fast asleep.

How did Pete help Tony? Who would you talk to if you felt afraid?

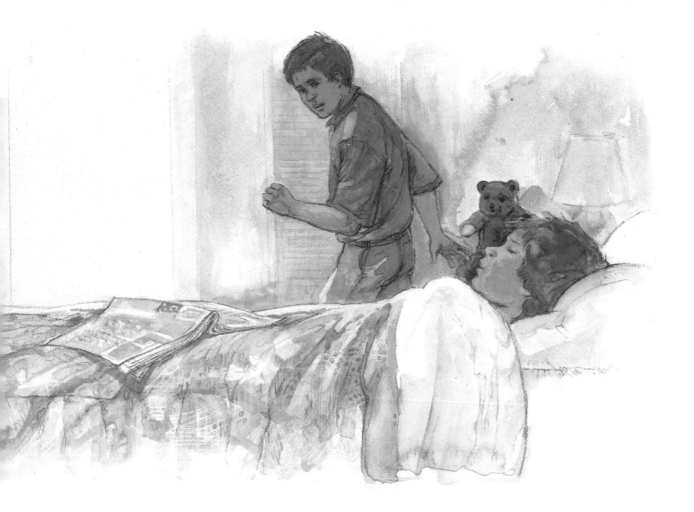

Feeling like Tony

Have you ever felt afraid, like Tony? Nearly everyone feels frightened sometimes. It feels worse when you know that there is nothing to be scared of. But you can't stop yourself being afraid.

It helps to talk

Fears grow when you keep them to yourself. The best thing to do if you feel afraid is to talk about it. Tell someone you trust. Don't be scared that other people will laugh at you. Only silly people laugh.

14

Feeling scared is natural

Sometimes there is a good reason to be scared. Some dogs do bite, sometimes people do slip on ice, teachers do get cross. Fear is natural. It is sensible to take care when you meet a stray dog and when you walk on icy streets. But there is no point in being scared for no reason.

Think about it

Read the stories in this book. Think about the people in the stories. Do you feel like them sometimes? Think what you do when you feel afraid. Think what is the best thing for you to do. Next time you feel scared, ask yourself some questions. Why am I scared? Can what I'm scared of happen? Who can I tell? Then talk to someone, just as Tony did.

Rosa's story

"Have a good day at school, Rosa!"

Rosa stood outside the school gates and waved to her mum. Soon the car was out of sight. Just then a loud voice called.

"There she is!"

Rosa started to run, but she was too late. Four big girls stood round her. Rosa felt very small. She was afraid.

"Give us your money," said one of the big girls. Rosa could feel the pound coin in her pocket. She closed her hand tightly around it.

"No," she said. The big girls came nearer.

"Come on. Give it to us - quickly," they said.

One of the girls grabbed Rosa's arm and squeezed hard. Rosa could feel her lip wobbling. She wanted to cry. She held out her hand and another girl snatched the coin away. Then the biggest girl gave Rosa a push.

"Don't tell or we'll hurt you," the girl shouted. Then the four bullies ran away.

How is Rosa feeling now?

Rosa hurried into her classroom. Mrs Young her teacher smiled at her.

"You're early, Rosa," said Mrs Young.

Rosa quickly got out her reading book. She pretended she was finishing a story. Really Rosa was thinking about the bullies. They had taken her dinner money. They had caught her last week too. Rosa thought about the big girls all morning.

At lunchtime Rosa felt sad.

"What's the matter?" asked her friend Jo. "Tell me." So Rosa told Jo what had happened.

"We must tell Mrs Young," said Jo. Rosa knew that Jo was right but she was still afraid.

"Let's share my packed lunch first," said Jo.

Rosa and Jo found Mrs Young in the classroom. Together they told their teacher all about the bullies.

"Can you tell me what they look like?" Mrs Young asked. Rosa remembered the biggest girl who'd grabbed her arm, and the one with the spiky hair.

"I know the girls you mean," said Mrs Young. "You did the right thing in telling me," she said. "Now you mustn't worry, I'll take care of those girls."

Do you think Rosa and Jo were right to tell Mrs Young? What do you think Mrs Young will say to the bullies?

After school, Jo waited until Rosa's mum arrived.
Two girls hurried past them.

"There go the bullies," whispered Rosa. But now the big girls didn't seem frightening. They had their heads down and they didn't look at Rosa.

"They're ashamed of themselves," said Jo.

Why isn't Rosa frightened now? How do you think the bullies are feeling?

Feeling like Rosa

The bullies knew Rosa was scared of them. They knew that they could make her give them money, and they tried to make her so afraid that she would never tell. Have you ever felt scared of someone, like Rosa? Do you know any bullies who get their own way by frightening others? Most bullies are older and stronger than the people they pick on. Some adults are bullies too.

Speak out!

Keeping quiet helps bullies. It gives them power. But you can take that power away, just by talking. The best thing to do if you feel like Rosa is to talk to someone who can help - your parents or a teacher. Don't help bullies by keeping them secret.

Simon's story

Simon was having fun. He was in the park with his friends. They were playing football and Simon's team was winning.

"Pass the ball Simon!" someone shouted.

Simon was just about to kick the ball. Just then a big black dog raced across the field. Simon left the ball and ran. The dog chased after him.

"Mum!" shouted Simon.

Simon threw himself at his mum.

"It's all right," she said. "He wanted to play, that's all. Look, he's gone now."

Simon watched the black dog trotting away.

At home, Simon's dad had some news.

"Here's a letter from Uncle Tom. He's coming to stay with us in two weeks' time."

"Great!" said Simon. "He's my favourite uncle."

"Now Simon," said his dad. "This time Uncle Tom's bringing his dog with him."

"But I'm scared of dogs!" shouted Simon. "Tell Uncle Tom we can't have a dog here!"

"You need to know more about dogs," said Simon's dad. "Then they won't seem so frightening."

How do you think Simon felt when he knew a dog was coming to stay?

That afternoon Simon and his dad went to the library.
They went to a shelf marked 'Pets'. Simon's dad
opened a big book and pointed to a yellow dog.

"Look," he said. "That's a labrador. It's the same
kind of dog as Uncle Tom's. Let's borrow this book,
Simon."

Simon looked through the book with his dad.
"How big is a labrador?" asked Simon.
"When it's standing up, its head would probably reach
your tummy," said Simon's dad. Simon groaned.
"I wish Uncle Tom had a kitten or a rabbit."

Simon and his dad looked at the book every evening after school. By Saturday Simon had learned a lot about labradors.

"We'd better do some extra shopping for Uncle Tom's visit," said Simon's mum. "I'll need your help, Simon. You know what dogs eat."

At the supermarket, Simon carefully lifted the tins of dog food from the shelves.

"What does Uncle Tom call his dog?" asked Simon.

"I think she's called Sheba," said his mum.

"Poor dog!" said Simon.

The day that Uncle Tom arrived, Simon woke up early. He couldn't wait! At last a car pulled up outside and Simon dashed to the door.

"Remember, don't jump around too much and get Sheba excited," warned Simon's dad. Simon ran up to Uncle Tom. He saw Sheba sitting in the back of the car. Her tail was wagging. She didn't look at all fierce.

While Uncle Tom told everyone about his drive down, Sheba looked round the house. She sniffed at Simon's football bag.

"She can smell your trainers!" said Simon's mum.

Simon watched Uncle Tom stroking Sheba.

"Give her a pat if you like," said Uncle Tom.

"Not yet," said Simon.

How do you think Simon feels now?

Simon and Uncle Tom took Sheba for a walk. They threw sticks and Sheba brought them back in her mouth. Simon enjoyed the game. Soon he was running ahead looking for new sticks. Then he heard Sheba panting close behind. Simon wasn't sure what to do. He ran faster and so did Sheba. Then Simon heard Uncle Tom shouting.

"Slow down, Simon! She's only playing."

Simon stopped running - and Sheba stopped too.

Why do you think Sheba is chasing Simon? What should Simon do?

"Did she frighten you?" asked Uncle Tom, puffing.

"Not really," said Simon, stroking Sheba's ears. "She just got excited."

Simon looked down at Sheba's silky head.

"I'm glad you brought Sheba to stay," he said. "I know more about dogs now."

"And when you're playing football and a strange dog joins in, what will you do?" asked Uncle Tom.

"I'll stand still until it goes away!" said Simon.

How did Sheba's visit help Simon?

Feeling like Simon

Have you ever felt scared of an animal, like Simon? Some people are scared of spiders or wasps or cats. Whenever they meet one they panic. Simon had to learn more about dogs. By getting to know more about the things he feared, Simon was able to relax. Of course, it makes sense to be careful when a strange dog bounds up to you. But it doesn't help to get upset. It's the same with any other fear - try not to panic. Think what you can do about your problem.

Feeling afraid

Think about the stories in this book. Tony, Rosa and Simon were each afraid of different things, and they each found someone to help them. If you say, "I'm afraid," someone will help you too.

Asking for help

It's often hard to tell someone else that you're afraid. But talking to someone you trust makes you feel stronger. You may have to ask for help, like Rosa. We all need help sometimes.

Keep trying

Rosa was lucky. Her teacher had time to listen. But if the first person you talk to can't help try again. Tell a neighbour or a friend about your fear. There is always someone who can help.

If you are feeling frightened or unhappy, don't keep it to yourself. Talk to an adult you can trust, like a parent or a teacher. If you feel really alone, you could telephone or write to one of these offices. Remember, there is always someone who can help.

Childline
Freephone 0800 1111
Address: Freepost 1111, London   N1 0BR

NSPCC Child Protection Line
Freephone 0800 181188

NCH Careline
Birmingham (021) 440 5970
Cardiff (0222) 229461
Glasgow (041) 221 6722
Glenrothes (0592) 759651
Leeds (0532) 456456
London (081) 514 1177
Luton (0582) 422751
Maidstone (0622) 56677
Preston (0772) 24006

NAYPIC
Especially for children who are in care
(061) 9534051